J914.4

2001

Modern Industrial World

France

Mick Dunford

Wayland

MODERN INDUSTRIAL WORLD

Austria	**Italy**
Benelux countries	**Japan**
Canada	**Portugal**
France	**Russia**
Germany	**South Africa**
Ireland	**Spain**
Israel	**Sweden**

Cover: *La Défense*, a famous piece of Paris architecture.
Title page: A line of volcanic *puys* in Auvergne is bathed in evening sunlight.
Contents page: Wine bottles stored in a cellar.

Series editor: Paul Mason
Series designer: Malcolm Walker

First published in 1994 by
Wayland (Publishers) Ltd
61 Western Road, Hove
East Sussex, BN3 1JD, England

© Copyright 1994 by Wayland (Publishers) Ltd

British Library Cataloguing in Publication Data
Dunford, Michael
   France. - (Modern Industrial World series)
   I. Title II. Series
   914.4

ISBN 0-7502-0988-7

Typeset by Kudos Design.
Printed in Italy by G. Canale & C. S.p.A. - Borgaro T.se - TURIN

Contents

Introduction	4
The development of modern France	6
Landscapes and land usage	10
Government in France	14
The Peoples of France	17
Work in France	21
Food, farming and rural life	26
Trade and industry	30
The transport system	34
The Paris megalopolis	36
Daily life	41
The future	44
Glossary	46
Further information	47
Index	48

Introduction

Competitors in the 1988 Tour de France speed through a field of sunflowers. The two-week race is the most famous cycling competition in the world. It covers the whole of France, as well as visiting other countries.

France is one of the oldest countries in Europe, and until the First World War it was a great political and military power. Today the French economy is the fifth largest in the world, and France is still a major international force, with a seat on the United Nations Security Council. France was also a founder member of the European Union.

France is famous for many things. The fashions of the Paris catwalks influence clothes designers around the world. Its chefs cook some of the world's greatest dishes. The wines, champagnes and cognacs of France are renowned the world over. France is home to the Tour de France cycle race; the Eiffel Tower; more than 300 different cheeses; brilliant novelists, painters and poets; great films, directors, actors and singers; and leading scientists and philosophers.

FRANCE AT A GLANCE
Total coastline: 6,200 kilometres.
Total land area: 552,000 square kilometres.
Highest mountain: Mont Blanc 4,807 metres.
Number of inhabitants: 56.6 million.
Life expectancy for men: 73 years.
Life expectancy for women: 81 years.
Currency: the franc (FF).

'Even in November, the cafe-terraces are filled with sunbathers enjoying their two-hour lunch break. . . while groups of old men play boules. The evenings are magical in the narrow streets and little squares of the old town, where the rose-pink facades of the buildings glow.' **From France Today by John Ardagh, 1990 edition.**

In spite of its worldwide economic, political and cultural impact, France is not a large country. Just under 57 million people live in mainland France. Another 1.6 million live in France's small and scattered overseas *départements* and territories. The people of France make up just over one per cent of the world's population. France occupies an even smaller proportion of the world's land area: 552,000 square kilometres, or 0.5 per cent.

The development of modern France

A scene of early trade in France shows sailing ships drawn up at the quayside in Bordeaux, one of France's main cities.

France lies between the early centres of European trade in northern Italy and Flanders (which is now a part of Belgium). As these centres of trade developed, so did France. From 1689-1815 and again in the nineteenth century France expanded overseas and created a vast colonial empire. The empire brought huge amounts of money to France, as the profits of colonial businesses were spent in the gambling houses and restaurants of Paris.

France was one of the world's richest and most powerful nations by the middle of the nineteenth century. But after the early development of modern industries, the economy and population grew more slowly than in most other advanced industrial countries. From 1820 to 1950 France's economy grew 3.9 times, while those of the sixteen most advanced countries grew 4.7 times. France's population also grew slowly, increasing 1.4 times, compared with 3.2 in the other developed countries.

Until the nineteenth century, industrial development was mostly limited to the northern borders and the area around Paris. This concentration of French industries in border areas was a problem for France, which was invaded three times between 1870 and 1944. For example, France lost Alsace-Lorraine to Prussia in 1870 and did not get it back until the end of the First World War.

THE FRENCH EMPIRE

During the nineteenth century the great European powers carved up the globe between them, taking control of huge areas of land. France was no exception.

The colonies were only one part of French overseas investment. In 1914 just 9 per cent of France's FF 45 billion of overseas investments were in its colonies. So even outside

At its height the French Empire was second in size only to Britain's and covered 12 million square kilometres of land. France still has many territories around the world, which are shown in this map.

French départements and territories overseas

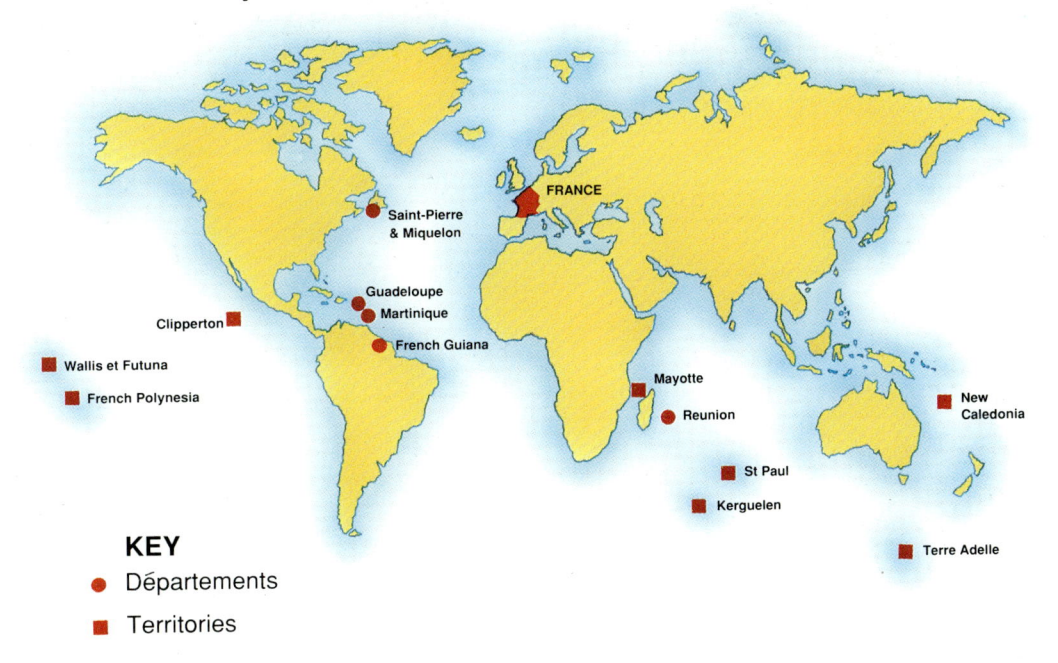

KEY
- Départements
- Territories

the borders of its colonies the power and influence of France were great. For example, the government of the Ottoman Empire borrowed huge amounts of money over the years: two-thirds of this was owed to French banks and money lenders.

A FARMING LAND
On the eve of the Second World War, in 1939, almost one-third of French people with jobs worked in agriculture. French industry and services had not grown enough to offer jobs to more than two-thirds of the workforce. In many rural areas life had changed little since the end of the nineteenth century. Farmers used few machines, and in the west of France in particular most farms were small and family-run. The countryside was dotted with small towns where farmers sold their goods at the market, and where there were small shops, small-scale industries, and a small-town middle class of traders, doctors and lawyers.

In 1940 France was dramatically defeated by Germany. One of the reasons for its defeat was its failure to modernize its industries as fast as Germany, which meant the French could not produce enough tanks, aircraft and guns to defend themselves.

LES TRENTE GLORIEUSES
In 1944 France was liberated from German occupation, but its economy had been devastated. A new government was formed by the different resistance groups that had fought

This painting, made in 1860, shows farm workers haymaking. Although by this time France's cities were growing bigger and industry was expanding, most of the population still worked on the land.

against the German occupiers. The new government began an industrialization campaign.

A welfare state was established, to provide everyone with an income in times of unemployment, health care in times of illness and education. To help modernize French industries the government began a famous economic planning system. Industries such as the Renault car company were nationalized, as were the four main banks and the main insurance companies. A thirty-year period of spectacular economic growth followed. The French call this era from 1946 to 1975 *les Trente Glorieuses* – 30 glorious years.

During *les Trente Glorieuses* France withdrew from most of its colonies. This process began in 1954 when French colonial forces were defeated at Dien-Bien-Phu in Vietnam. In Algeria, another French colony, the nine million inhabitants included one million white settlers of French nationality, called *colons*. They persuaded the French government to oppose independence for Algeria, and a bitter eight-year conflict ensued. This conflict brought France itself to the verge of a civil war. In 1962 it ended when the French government granted Algeria independence and brought most of the *colons* back to France.

Today France plays an important role in international affairs in a post-colonial world, and is an advanced industrial nation. But like other advanced countries it has had great difficulty in adapting to the slower growth and unemployment of the years since the mid-1970s.

Above *A French oil refinery.*

Below *River barges such as these are used to transport goods.*

Landscapes and land usage

All France's frontiers are natural except those in the north-east. Seas, mountains or major rivers separate it from most of its neighbours. France has 6,200 kilometres of coastline, on the North Sea, the English Channel, the Atlantic and the Mediterranean. A short sea crossing separates France from Britain, and it shares frontiers with six other countries: Belgium, Luxembourg, Germany, Switzerland, Italy and Spain. The river Rhine forms a part of France's frontier with Germany.

PLAINS

Across northern Europe there are great, sweeping plains broken by low hills. These plains extend into north-eastern France and merge with the fertile lands of the Paris Basin and with the Aquitaine Basin in the south-west.

Above A spectacular sunrise in the French Alps above the town of Chamonix.

MOUNTAINS

In the uplands of Brittany, the forest-covered Ardennes, the wooded lands of Vosges and the Massif Central are ancient hills. These were once giant, towering peaks, but over 250 million years they have been flattened by the wind and the rain into smaller mountains. In the south the limestone plateaux of the Causses are cut by the spectacular Tarn gorges. To the east of the Causses are the spectacular pine and chestnut-covered granites and schists of the Cévennes.

On the southern borders are younger mountains – a mere 65 million years old. The Pyrenees lie on the border with Spain, and the Jura and French Alps separate France from Switzerland and Italy. The Pyrenees reach 3,404 metres, but the highest peaks are in the Alps: Mont Blanc reaches 4,807 metres and is Europe's tallest mountain.

RIVERS

Three great rivers cross the northern and western plains. The Seine passes through Paris on its route to the sea at Le Havre, and barges carry goods to and from the capital.

The Loire is the longest French river. It flows for 1,020 kilometres from the Massif Central to the Atlantic, which it meets at the city of Nantes.

The Garonne originates in the Pyrenees and is joined by the Dordogne, whose source lies in the Massif Central, before it reaches the Atlantic near Bordeaux.

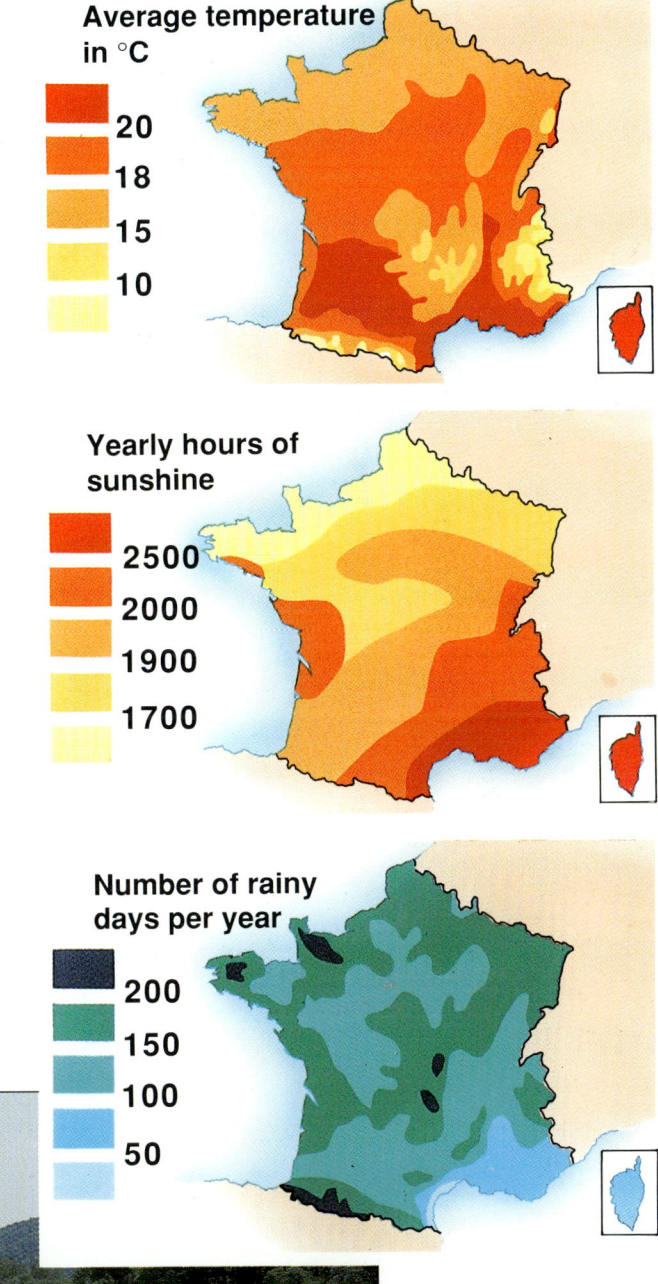

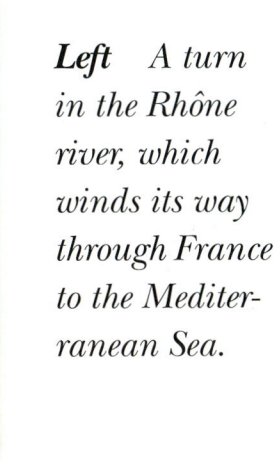

Average temperature in °C
- 20
- 18
- 15
- 10

Yearly hours of sunshine
- 2500
- 2000
- 1900
- 1700

Number of rainy days per year
- 200
- 150
- 100
- 50

Left A turn in the Rhône river, which winds its way through France to the Mediterranean Sea.

France's fourth great river is the Rhône. The Rhône originates in Switzerland and passes through Lake Geneva, huddled under Mont Blanc. It is joined by the Saône at Lyon. In places the river is dammed to produce electricity and water for industrial use. As the Rhône reaches the Mediterranean it crosses a delta called the Camargue, a land of shallow lakes, marshes, white horses, wild flamingos and black bulls.

WEATHER AND CLIMATE
Overall there is a clear north-south divide in the French weather. In the north there is less sunshine and more rain, though the weather is dryer further from the sea. In the south summers are hot and winters are warmer than in the north. Summers are dryer in Mediterranean France than in Aquitaine in the south-west, which is more humid.

In the south-east, near the Mediterranean, the winters are mild and the summers are hot and dry. This leads to fires in areas of forest and scrubland. Sometimes, as the seasons change a cold northern wind called the Mistral blows down the Rhône-Saône Valley for days on end.

In Brittany and Normandy, winds and depressions sweep in from the Atlantic Ocean, bringing plenty of rain. There are few high mountains in this part of France, so nothing stops the rainclouds being blown right across the region.

In the east the influence of weather conditions in central and eastern Europe is great. The winters are cold and the sky is often clear, while the summers are hot and summer storms are common.

LAND USE
The vast areas of rural land and forest between the major cities are very varied. In the north the plains are covered

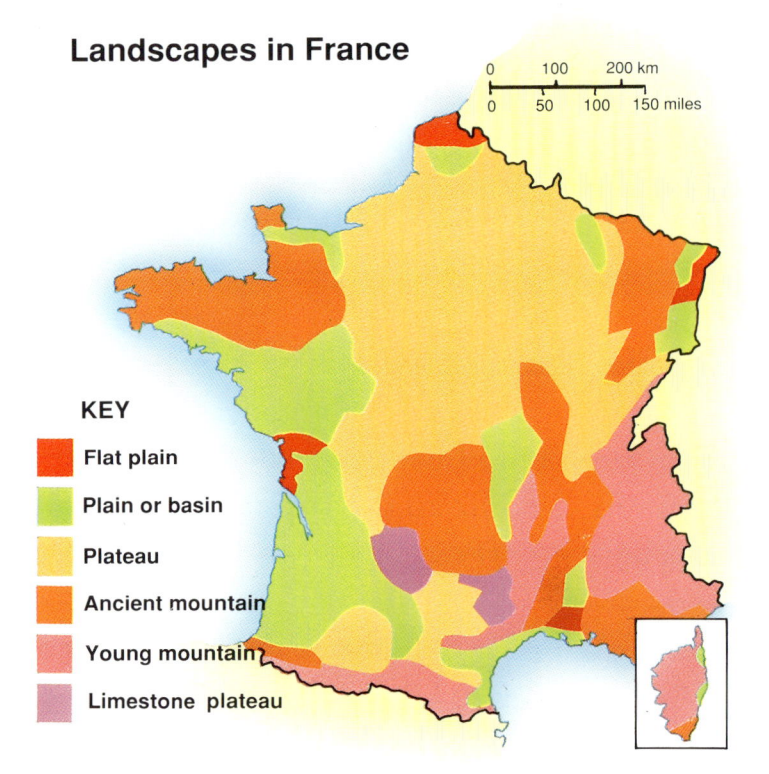

Landscapes in France

KEY
- Flat plain
- Plain or basin
- Plateau
- Ancient mountain
- Young mountain
- Limestone plateau

12

with large open fields on which cereals and sugar beet grow. In the west the fields are smaller, and animal raising is more important than crop growing. In some parts of the Massif Central stone walls separate the fields and sheep are frequently reared. In the Mediterranean fruits and olives are grown.

CITIES

Some parts of France are highly urbanized. Paris is in the middle of a fertile river basin. There are other large urban areas around Lille in the mining and industrial area of the Nord, and in the coal and iron mining areas in the north of Lorraine. Lyon is a great commercial and industrial city at the confluence of the Rhône and Saône rivers. Marseille is France's main Mediterranean port. Toulouse developed on the banks of the Garonne as the capital of an agricultural region, and Bordeaux, Nantes and Le Havre developed on the estuaries of three of France's great rivers.

The town of Lyon, shown here, is one of France's largest cities. It lies where the Rhône and Saône rivers meet, and is a great trading centre.

POPULATION DENSITY

Between the large cities lie rural areas where the population density is much lower. In France as a whole the density of population is between a half and a third of that of most neighbouring countries. Because there are fewer people, there are lower levels of air and water pollution, and there is less damage to forests from acid rain.

Government in France

Voters on Réunion, a French island territory, welcome the French president François Mitterand.

NATIONAL GOVERNMENT

France is a republic rather than a monarchy. In a republic the head of state is elected. There have been five republics in France since the 1789 Revolution removed the monarchy. With the creation of each republic a new constitution was written. The present republic – the Fifth Republic – was established by General de Gaulle in 1958.

France is governed by a number of ministries, such as the Ministry of Economic Affairs and Finance, which have their own civil servants. Each minister has a cabinet of personal assistants and advisers. As well as the ministries, there are groups of officials who work for major government bodies known as *grands corps*. Most leading politicians, civil servants, managers of large companies, and heads of financial institutions are trained in schools known as *grandes écoles.* These are special institutions of higher education that exist alongside the universities. Getting into a *grande école* can be very difficult.

REGIONAL AND LOCAL GOVERNMENT

The structure of French local government dates from the years following the 1789 Revolution. Until recently the national government controlled education, the police, justice, social security, the health system, the public services and local government. There were two tiers of local government. At the lowest level there were 36,000 communes, which varied from small communes of a few hundred inhabitants to large cities. Above the communes there were 96 *départements* headed by very powerful government officials called prefects.

In 1981 a socialist government was elected. In 1982 it introduced the Deferre Law. The aim of the Deferre Law

Another election rally, this time in the Place de la République in the heart of Paris.

Bright flags decorate the Mairie (town hall) of a town in Limousin, during a local fête. The Mairie, or Hôtel de Ville as they are sometimes called, is the headquarters of the commune. The communes can be tiny villages or huge cities such as Paris.

was to move government closer to the people and to make it more democratic, and it led to major changes in French government. Now there are three tiers of local government with different responsibilities, though they share some jobs (road construction and education, for example).

THE COMMUNES

The 36,000 communes are each headed by a mayor. The offices for each commune are in the *Hôtel de Ville* or *Mairie* (Town Hall). Communes provide a variety of local services, for example local roads, schools and urban public transport. In addition communes have responsibilities for urban planning, environmental protection and local economic development. It is the mayor who grants permission for new buildings.

THE DEPARTEMENTS

There are 95 of these. In each *département* there is an elected *départemental* council, whose members are called *conseillers généraux*. The presidents of the *départements* took over the powers of the old prefects, so now an elected official does the job that used to be done by an unelected one. The *départements* are responsible for social assistance.

THE REGIONS

There are 22 regions, run by elected regional councils, which have existed since 1986. The regions have responsibilities for major roads, economic development, secondary education, vocational training and cultural affairs.

The peoples of France

An open-air market in the rue Mouffetard, Paris. Among the crowd are many of France's different people: Basques; immigrants from Africa, the Pacific and the Caribbean; Alsatians; Celts and Gauls.

Because it borders so many other countries, France has been invaded many times, and has done its own share of invading. As a result the people of France are very diverse in origin. In the Roman era most of the inhabitants were Gallic people, who came from Central Europe but mixed with the Romans. Other communities also existed. In the south-west on the mountain borders with Spain there were ancient Basque communities. Brittany was populated by Celts (as were Britain and Ireland). In Normandy were the descendants of Viking invaders from Scandinavia. Flemish people settled in the north-west, while the people of Alsace are Germanic. More recently people from the old French colonies in Africa, Asia and the Caribbean have also come to live in France.

In 1990 France had 56.6 million inhabitants. At present the population is growing slowly, but faster than in most other large European countries. The number of inhabitants is expected to reach 60 million in the first years of the next century.

At present French women have on average two children. Almost all children reach adulthood, so the number of people born in each generation is sufficient to replace their parents when they die. The increase in population comes mainly from the fact that French people are living longer.

Attitudes towards having children have changed: almost one in three French children is born outside of marriage. Women wait longer to have children. They delay having children for several reasons: some study for longer; others wait until they have well-paid jobs and good homes. Women also leave a larger gap between children so that they can continue with their careers.

'The main body of (France's Vietnamese) immigrants arrived at the end of the Vietnam war. They went to live in the high-rise flats that had just been finished off the Place de l'Italie... No ghetto, but a town within a town, a French Chinatown where the desire to be assimilated is obvious.'
From 'Chinatown Quotidien' in L'Evénement du Jeudi, February 1994.

Immigrant children stick their heads up through holes in the roof of their house.

A patisserie owned and run by people from Tunisia, in the Latin Quarter of Paris. In the cities especially, French people can enjoy foods from many different parts of the world just by walking for a few minutes down the road.

IMMIGRANTS

Many people migrate to France from other parts of the world. Some of these people are French citizens from North Africa, West Africa, Cambodia, Laos and Vietnam. The colour of their skins, their features, their religions, and their beliefs and values differ, but all of them are French.

Some of the people who move to France are foreigners. In 1990 there were 3.6 million foreigners in France. Most come from three countries in North Africa: Morocco, Algeria and Tunisia. There are also large numbers of people from Portugal, Spain, Italy and Britain living in France.

EXPANDING CITIES

Most French people live in or near a number of large cities. In three areas the populations are growing especially quickly as people move there to work or study. Many young people are attracted to the Paris area, with its night clubs, bars, restaurants, theatres, museums and cinemas. People are also moving to the south-east, especially the sunny Mediterranean coast, and also to the area around Toulouse and Bordeaux in the south-west.

Modern architecture - known locally as the Camemberts, after a famous kind of round cheese - springs up out of old land at Noisy le Grand on the outskirts of Paris. The area has been targeted for development by the French government, which encourages businesses to move there to provide people with work.

Paris to small towns in the Paris Basin, the west and the centre-west. The jobs that were created were taken by former agricultural workers and by women, who had worked mainly in the home.

After 1974 there were fewer and fewer industrial jobs available: factories were closed, land was left derelict and unemployment increased, especially in the old industrial areas in the north and east.

THE GROWTH OF SERVICES

Since the Second World War there has been an explosion of jobs in shops and offices. In 1990 three out of every four women in work and one in every two men worked in services. Most of these jobs were in large cities, though many of the people who work in the city live in suburbs, which have spread into the surrounding countryside.

THE RISE OF UNEMPLOYMENT

Les Trente Glorieuses ended almost twenty years ago. Today there are not enough jobs, and in 1993 more than 2.5 million people were unemployed. The people who suffer most from unemployment are clerks, shop and manual workers, young people who did not do well at school, and the children of immigrants.

URBAN DECAY

In many cities there are deprived areas where there is a combination of unemployment, derelict land, decaying housing and crime. In the 1980s there were some experimental government-supported schemes to renovate more than 140 poor housing estates. The French government is continuing to try to improve the situation for its poorest people.

DIFFERENCES IN WEALTH

Most people have become much richer since the war, but there are big differences in wealth between manual workers, who earn comparatively little, and well-paid doctors, lawyers and accountants. Men also generally earn more than women.

Above   The financial headquarters of Renault, the French car and truck manufacturer, at Noisy le Grand.

More modern architecture at Noisy le Grand, this time homes for workers.

23

THE SENSITIVE SUBURBS

At the end of *Les Trente Glorieuses*, many industries declined, so there was high unemployment. Those affected were mainly unskilled workers, unqualified young people and the children of immigrants. They lived mostly in the centres of large cities, in areas of low-cost houses which had been developed in the 1960s and early 1970s. In France these low-cost housing schemes are called HLM (*habitation à loyer modéré*). They are areas of high youth unemployment. For many years they had been neglected by the government, and became very run down.

These areas first hit the headlines in the early 1980s, when riots at Vénissieux in Lyon destroyed most of the centre of the high-rise estate of Les Minguettes. In the hot summer of 1985 there were new disturbances in the eastern communes of Lyon. These riots led to the formation of two important left-wing organizations that had direct links to President Mitterand. *SOS Racisme*, led by Harlem Désir, concentrates on organizing protests, especially over education policy. *Banlieues 89* is led by the architect Roland Castro.

Banlieues 89, backed by the government, renovated more than 140 low-cost estates, including Les Minguettes and the Mas du Taureau block in Vaulx-en-Vélin. The blocks

'*Don't let's sit around and moan. Complaining is a sterile occupation. Let's make the racists look really corny, and build a quarantine line around them that no one will be able to break through.*' **Harlem Désir, SOS Racisme leader, 1985.**

Although incomes from work differ, the government sets minimum wages, so low pay is less of a problem than in a number of other European countries. Also there is an

Local people attend the funeral of one the inhabitants of Vaulx-en-Vélin in October 1990.

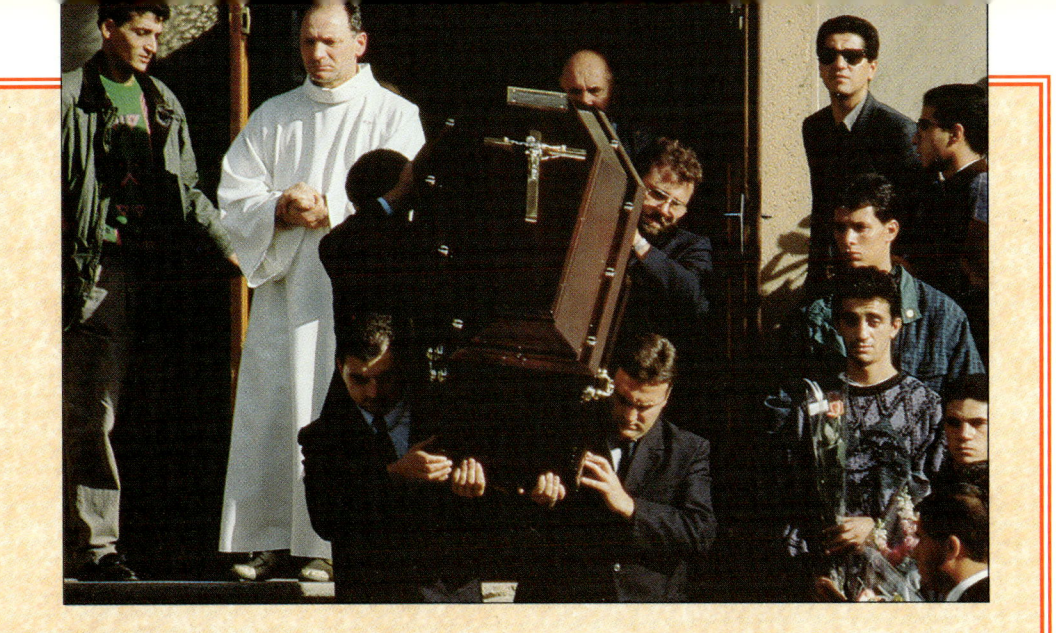

and towers have been made to look more attractive, shops and cafes have been built, and road and rail access has been improved. In Vaulx-en-Vélin, for example, the blocks were repainted, two thousand five hundred homes were renovated, houses were constructed to make the landscape more interesting, and shops and a library were built.

In October 1990 there were serious riots in Vaulx-en-Vélin. The government responded by introducing another urban renewal programme. At a December 1990 meeting of *Banlieues 89* in Lyon, President Mitterand announced that there would soon be a Minister for Urban Renewal. New laws would force the richest urban areas to give some of their income to the 400 poorest. Soon after, the new minister, Michel Delebarre, said that if any of the wealthy areas refused to help, people from the poorer areas would be moved into the richer ones.

'"What are we angry about? We're angry about everything," said a girl standing with a large group of friends in front of the smashed windows of the local shopping centre. "We want justice and we want it now. Otherwise we'll be out again tonight for another rampage."

'"This could have happened anywhere. Things are so bad that it only takes one spark to light the fire," Francis Parny, the deputy mayor, said. "We understand why all these young people feel hard done by."' **Guardian, *18 March 1994*.**

---

advanced social security system. This provides people with an income when they lose their job, have time away from work through sickness, or retire.

Food, farming and

France uses almost twice as much agricultural land – 30.4 million hectares – as Britain and Italy, and almost three times as much as West Germany. But the amount of agricultural land is decreasing: farmland on the edges of towns is used to construct houses, shops and factories. Some fields and farms are simply abandoned. Some is reforested – more than one quarter of France is covered by forests.

France is the biggest producer of agricultural goods in Europe, and produces a huge variety of different foodstuffs. Only the USA exports more food than France. Wine, cereals, meat, butter, eggs, sugar and potatoes are all sold overseas, and French farmers produce an extraordinary range of high quality products.

A hillside village and terraced vineyards in the Pyrenees, in the south-west of France. Winemaking is a major industry in France: millions of bottles are sold, many abroad.

rural life

THE FARMING REVOLUTION

In the last forty years there has been a revolution in French farming. In the early 1950s over 30 per cent of the workforce worked in agriculture, but farms were very inefficient. Most were small – on average 15 hectares. Fifty-six per cent of farms had less than 10 hectares of cultivable land. There was little farm machinery, farm incomes were low, rural homes were ill-equipped and few children from agricultural areas went on to further education.

Then more machines began to appear on farms. Farming became more scientific as genetic selection, fertilizers and computers started to be used. Enormous increases in output were recorded. Small farms joined together to form cooperatives: groups of farmers joined together to buy machinery, for example, which was then shared. Employment fell and part-time farming increased.

Now, there are large variations from one region to another. At present three main types of agricultural landscape can be identified:

GRANDE CULTURE

Grande Culture is large-scale farming. Most takes place in the old open field areas of the Paris Basin, and in the north and east. In these areas, people live in villages and small towns. Farms are large and produce mainly cereals, and farm incomes are high.

FARMING IN FRANCE

Agricultural land: 30.4 million hectares
Income from crops and animals is equal
1.5 million people work on farms

Land use in France

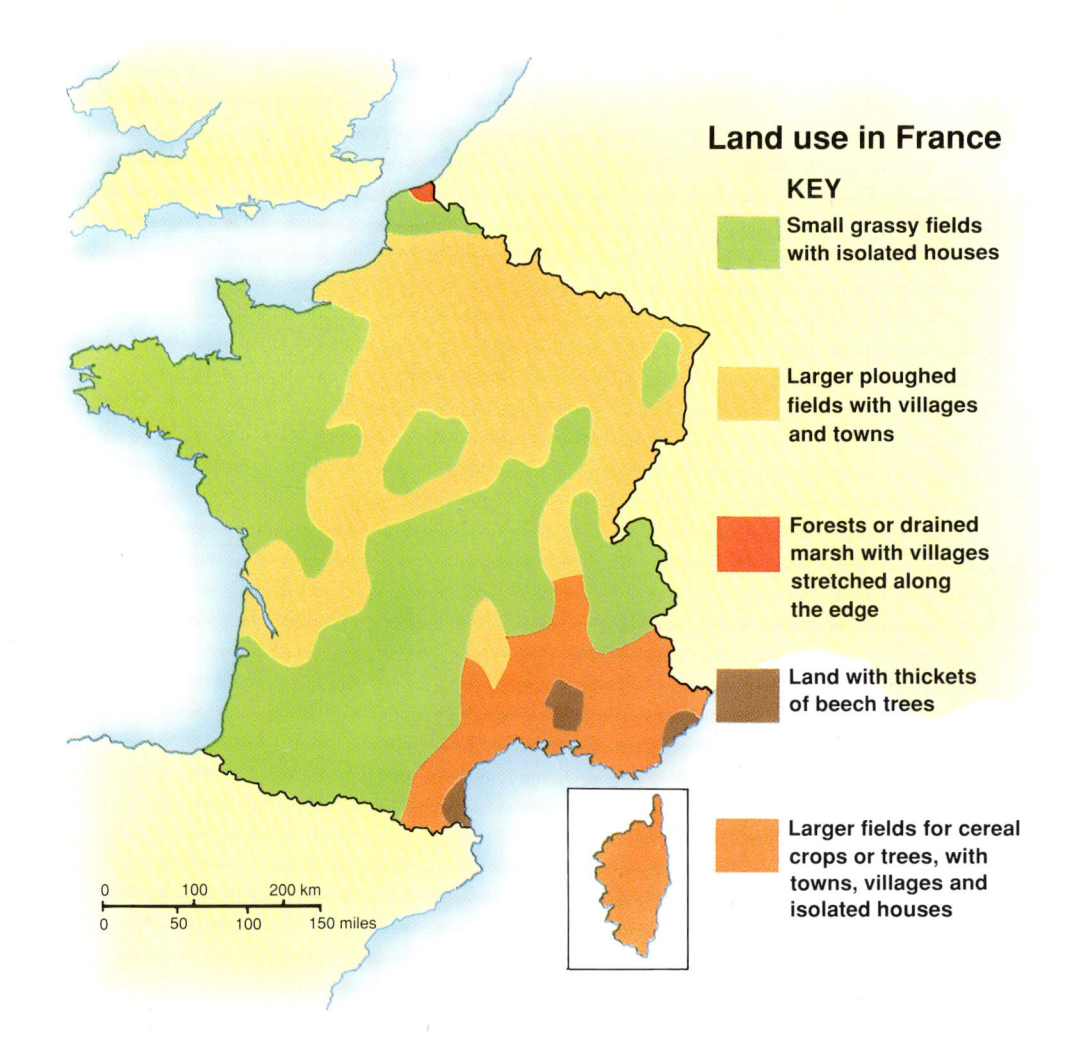

KEY

- Small grassy fields with isolated houses
- Larger ploughed fields with villages and towns
- Forests or drained marsh with villages stretched along the edge
- Land with thickets of beech trees
- Larger fields for cereal crops or trees, with towns, villages and isolated houses

BOCAGE

In Normandy and the west enclosed – or *bocage* – landscapes are common. These have isolated farms and small hamlets, and the fields are surrounded by hedges. Most farmers raise animals to produce milk, meat or both. Similar types of landscape are found in the Massif Central.

In Brittany especially there is a strong emphasis on intensive factory methods of rearing pigs and poultry.

THE MEDITERRANEAN

In Mediterranean areas there are terraced hillsides that have been abandoned to scrub or forest. But away from the coast are areas where cereals are grown, as well as vines and tree crops such as olives. The irrigated coastal plains are used to grow flowers, fruit and vines. Farms are normally small, and farmers less wealthy than in other parts of France.

'The French use 60,000 tonnes of mustard per year, that is one kilo per person. For six centuries Dijon has been the mustard capital of France. The Dukes of Burgundy would never travel without mustard in their baggage... In the eighteenth century, Maille – the King's vinegar maker – invented twenty-four recipes for mustard.'
From an article by Jean Ferniot in L'Evénement du Jeudi, *March 1994.*

The post-war mechanization of French agriculture had a major effect. The importance of farming in French society has declined. Today agriculture and food processing industries account for just 7 per cent of the economy. In 1990 there were just 1.5 million farmers, family helpers and farm labourers compared with 2.75 million in 1970. Despite this decline in numbers, French farmers are still a significant political force in rural areas, for two reasons. First, they are an important source of votes for right-wing political parties. Second, French farmers often take to the streets to defend their interests.

The US government argues that restrictions on the import of food to Europe should be removed, so that US farmers will be able to sell their products there. If the Americans do get these trade restrictions removed food prices may fall. But at the same time small farmers will lose their livelihood. Many French farmers are strongly opposed to the US proposals. The French government is also anxious about the future of farming, because agriculture accounts for a large share of French exports. If French farmers do go out of business because of cheap imports, they will not be exporting products to other countries, and the government will lose overseas earnings.

A terraced vineyard in Provence in south-east France. Some of the vines are over forty years old. Although agriculture has declined in France, wine-making is still an important activity.

Trade and industry

A nuclear power station sits in a beautiful valley. The French government has been building nuclear power stations for over twenty years in an attempt to reduce France's need to import coal and oil.

One of the most striking changes in France since the Second World War has been its dramatic modernization. During the *Trente Glorieuses* industries such as steel, textiles and shipbuilding remained important, and at the same time a whole crop of newer industries grew. Electrical household goods such as refrigerators, washing machines and television sets; cars; gas, water and electricity; and telecommunications were all developed to meet the needs of modern urban life. France also became a major producer of guns, rockets and military aircraft.

After 1973 many of the older industries such as steel, textiles and shipbuilding got smaller. Jobs were also lost in the car industry, as companies began to use industrial robots. The government tried – often successfully – to create more jobs by investing in high-technology industries such as telecommunications, high-speed trains, aerospace and nuclear power.

ENERGY SOURCES IN FRANCE			
	1973	1987	1991
Coal	17.3	9.7	7.5
Oil	2.2	3.7	3.4
Natural gas	6.3	3.2	2.9
Nuclear	3.3	59.0	73.6
Renewable energy	2.0	4.0	4.2
Other sources	10.7	16.2	13.8

Above French energy. The units are equivalent to 1,000,000 tonnes of oil.

Below Primary industries depend on raw materials such as iron ore or grapes. Secondary industries use these raw materials: making steel or wine are examples.

Industry in France

KEY
- Services and primary
- Services
- Secondary and services
- Secondary
- Primary and secondary
- Primary

ENERGY RESOURCES AND NUCLEAR POWER

France has almost no oil and very little natural gas. Its coal reserves are only small, and produce less and less coal each year. In 1973 the world price of oil went up, and the French government decided to try to find ways for France to produce its own energy. Nuclear power stations were built all over France, despite strong protests from environmental groups and others. Their concerns were dismissed, and today the nuclear power industry produces about 30 per cent of French energy needs.

SERVICE INDUSTRIES

Increasing numbers of French people work in service industries, instead of manufacturing industries. Service industries provide services, such as entertainment or public transport, rather than goods. There are some three million service firms in France: restaurants, car workshops, TV companies, hotels, schools and advertising agencies among them.

Because they need people nearby to sell their services to, most service industries set up in areas where a lot of people live: cities and large towns. In the countryside there are few services, and people sometimes decide to move towards the city. As the population falls, shops and schools close, and transport services get worse. The rural areas become even less attractive to live in.

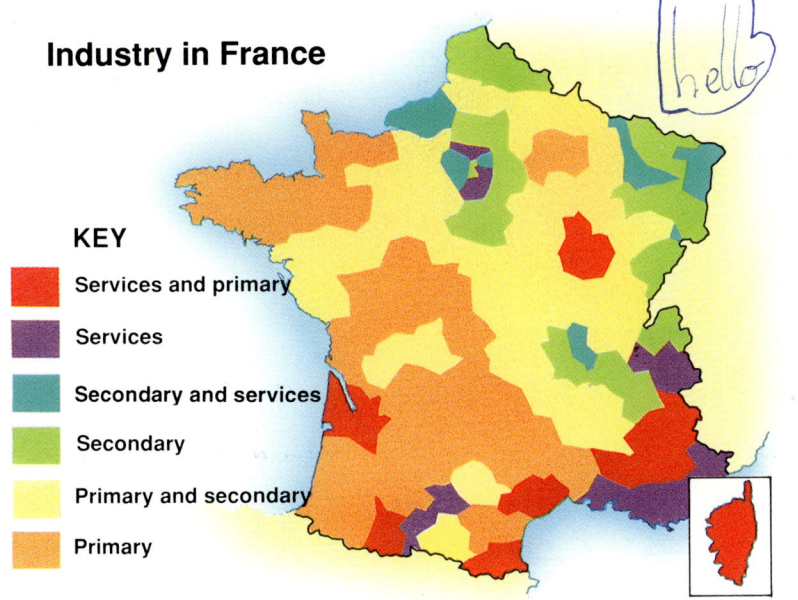

TOURISM AND LEISURE

Every year millions of people from other countries visit France on holiday. and French people now

31

INDUSTRY IN TOULOUSE

AEROSPACE INDUSTRIES

French industries are concentrated in the biggest cities. Paris is the most important, but there are others dotted around France. Toulouse is one of these.

Toulouse began to develop between the First and Second World Wars. The government decided then that the aircraft-making factories should be in the south-west corner of the country, far from Germany. Germany had already invaded France twice in the last fifty years, and was soon to do so again. After 1968, other similar industries moved to Toulouse: the National Centre for Space Research, and universities that specialized in aerospace engineering and research centres.

Other companies have continued the movement to Toulouse, hoping to take advantage of the skills of the local workers. The city continues to expand: the number of people working in the space industry went from 1,500 employees at the start of the 1980s to 6,500 in 1990. Toulouse is a leading centre for the French and European space programmes: satellites launched by rockets, such as Ariane, are built in Toulouse.

AIRBUS

Airbus Industrie, which makes the Airbus range of passenger aircraft, employs 11,500 people in the Toulouse area. It competes with huge

Airbus aircraft outside the Toulouse factory in which they were built.

have enough money to travel around the country in their spare time. Winter sports such as skiing are popular, and the sunshine of the Mediterranean coast attracts summer visitors. Millions of francs in foreign currency pour into French accounts each year from holidaymakers.

The northern French Alps are one of the most popular

US firms such as Boeing and McDonnell-Douglas. The first plane Airbus built was the A300, which is used by Air France and most other major European airlines. Recently the company also launched the A320, which is one of the world's most advanced passenger planes.

OTHER INDUSTRIES

Two other industries are very important to Toulouse. Ten thousand people work in the electronics, industrial robot and computer software industries. Large firms such as the American microchip manufacturer Motorola and the French firm Thomson live next door to small and medium-sized local firms. There is also a long-established chemicals and powders industry.

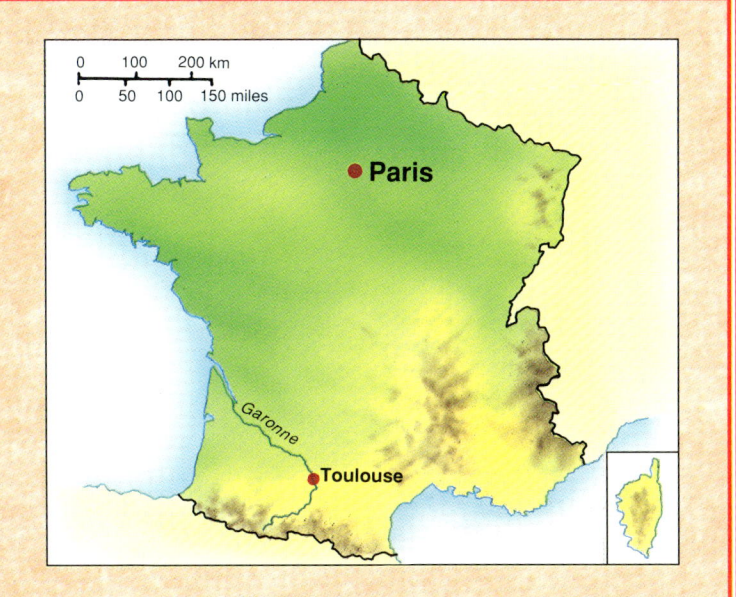

Industrial development can only occur if there is sufficient skilled labour. The development of these industries also involved the development of education, training and research. At present there are 51,000 students in three universities in Toulouse. There are also 7,000 researchers in the city.

Ariane, the European space rocket, is launched in French Guiana in the Caribbean. Many of the parts were made in Toulouse.

winter sports areas in Europe. In 1924, 1968 and 1992 the Winter Olympics took place in this part of France, and each year the slopes are crowded with skiers. But even more people visit the Mediterranean coastline. Many other parts of France attract vistors who wish to spend time by the sea, in the countryside or in the mountains.

33

The transport system

THE TRAIN A GRANDE VITESSE

The French transport system is among the most modern and efficient in the world. The world-famous high-speed train (*Train à Grande Vitesse – TGV*) and the métro trains used in Paris, Lyon, Lille and Marseille are all built in France.

The French railway system was nationalized – bought by the government – in 1937. Since then the government has almost constantly invested money in its railway network. Today, most passengers travel on electrified lines. The service people get from SNCF amazes visitors from other countries: the trains arrive on time, and are comfortable and quick. They are also safe: a hundred times safer than cars.

Trains do less damage to the environment than cars. Electric trains do not pollute the atmosphere as much and use less than half the energy of aeroplanes or cars.

Lines using trains that reach 300 kilometres per hour have been built to the west, the south-west and the Channel tunnel. One day the whole of western Europe may be linked by a high-speed train network. It will be far quicker to go from city to city: if Britain builds a fast link to London from the Channel tunnel, it will only take 2 hours 45 minutes to get there from Paris. The journey now takes over five hours.

A TGV train races along the railway line.

TRAIN TIMES FROM PARIS			
	1990	1995*	2010*
Barcelona	8.45	8.05	4.30
London	5.15	3.00	2.45
Brussels	2.30	2.30	1.20
Frankfurt		5.50	3.10
Milan		7.15	4.15

*estimated times
Train journey times shorten greatly as the new high-speed routes come into operation.

TRAFFIC

In French cities especially, congestion is a serious problem. Traffic moves very slowly, traffic jams are frequent and the way is often half-blocked by someone who has parked illegally. On some larger roads there is also heavy traffic. This is because a lot of goods are transported by road.

In particularly busy areas, such as the Rhône and Saône valleys, the amount of heavy goods traffic has increased sharply. Heavy goods traffic is also great along the routes to and from the Fréjus and Mont Blanc tunnels, which lead through the Alps to Italy. On these roads almost half the traffic is already made up of heavy goods vehicles.

The French already move more goods by rail than many other countries. In future rail and water transport of goods may offer the only solution to increased congestion and pollution.

'Parisians drive more aggressively. . . (In) the Ville de Paris (the city proper, within the gates). . . apart from the boulevards, most streets are narrow and canyon-like. This congestion leads to tensions in daily life that the Parisians' restless, intolerant, self-willed temperament is particularly ill-suited to coping with.' **From France Today by John Ardagh, 1990 edition.**

A Parisian traffic jam.

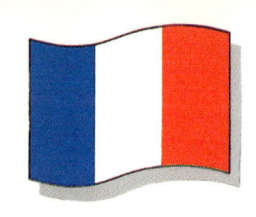

The Paris megalopolis

The heart of Paris seen from the air. The shiny, hollow cube in the middle of the picture is part of La Défense. At the other end of the straight road leading from it is the Arc de Triomphe. The layout of Paris was designed in the nineteenth century by Baron Haussman.

Paris is a city whose 9.3 million people come from all over the world. Two million live in the city itself, which is bordered by the *Boulevard Périphérique*. This is a road that runs along the line of the old city walls which were destroyed after the First World War. The rest of Paris's population lives in the suburbs.

PARIS AT A GLANCE
Number of inhabitants: 9.3 million. Area of metropolitan region: 2,118 square kilometres. Main airports: Charles de Gaulle and Orly. Most famous monument: Eiffel Tower (built 1887-89).

PARIS'S REVOLUTIONARY HISTORY

The history of Paris is littered with revolutions: in the century from 1775 to 1875 there were four main ones, with smaller revolutions contained within the big ones. Paris was where the course of French history was decided and where there was a tradition of people taking to the streets to express their dissatisfaction with the government.

1789 The first and most famous revolution took place in 1789. On one side was a bourgeoisie of bankers, industrialists, merchants, lawyers and doctors. On the other were aristocrats, many powerful priests and a king who claimed to rule by Divine Right.

The bourgeoisie demanded more power, which the old order would not give up. A revolution started: a National Assembly was set up, and the Bastille, a fortress used as a political prison, was captured by a mob of citizens. In August the Assembly proclaimed the famous Declaration of the Rights of Man – personal freedom, equality and fraternity – which has underpinned most subsequent discussions of human rights. Then in 1792 France was proclaimed a republic, and the king was executed.

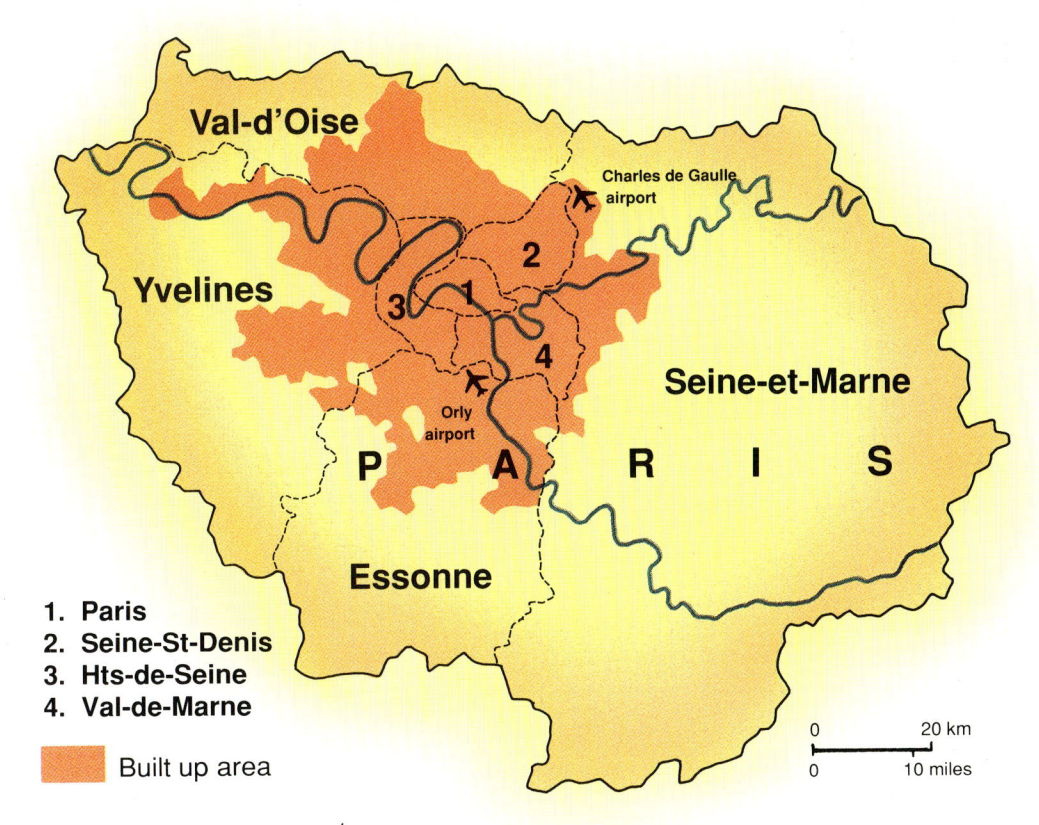

1. Paris
2. Seine-St-Denis
3. Hts-de-Seine
4. Val-de-Marne

Built up area

1848 In 1815 the monarchy was restored by the group of European powers that had defeated the French general Napoleon. But by 1848 there was another revolution. Riots in Paris forced the abdication of King Louis-Philippe and a new republic was proclaimed.

Elections led to a more conservative group winning power. In June another uprising in Paris was violently put down by the conservatives and 10,000 were killed.

1870 In 1870 France was defeated by Prussia (now part of Germany). A provisional government was set up in Bordeaux, headed by Thiers. The people of Paris refused to surrender to the Prussians, who Thiers had agreed could enter the city. In 1871 the Paris Commune was set up. Thiers's government sent troops to crush the revolt, and after bitter fighting in the streets the capital was recaptured for the government.

1968 During the 1960s there were more young people in France than ever before, but there were too few schools, houses, hospitals and recreational facilities to go around. By the end of the decade people's feelings were starting to boil over into anger. In May 1968 student protests met with a brutal police response. Suddenly all those who had complaints against the government were sparked into action. In Nantes a workers' committee ruled the city for a week. Nine million people went on strike. Then people in medicine, education, the media and the arts began to give vent to their grievances. Government forces clashed most fiercely with students and left-wingers in the Latin Quarter of Paris, where there were running battles in the streets. The government survived, but only by giving in to some of the demands made by the protesters and using force to regain control of the areas it had lost.

PARIS TODAY
Paris has sprawled out beyond the boundary of the *Boulevard Périphérique,* outside which most of the population lives. Some live in wonderful old towns such as Versailles, where

Les Invalides, one of Paris's oldest buildings, bathes in evening sunshine.

> *'Montparnasse is scarcely recognizable nowadays, with its giant Franprix supermarket, and its huge flat-sided cube sculptures. In Montparnasse... Cheap clothes, fast food and decibels have cluttered up the pavements, which smell of chips and reek of swindling.'* **From 'C'était hier...' L'Express Magazine, *April 1992*.**

Louis XIV held his court in the seventeenth century. Some live in suburbs built between the wars, in houses surrounded by gardens. Many live in five new towns developed in the 1970s and 1980s. But many others live in high-rise concrete jungles built in the 1950s and 1960s to provide quick homes for the people who were flooding into Paris. Among the most famous of these are Sarcelles (which has had a psychological condition named after it) and La Courneuve, where there are 4,000 identical apartments. To the west of Paris are much better apartments with local services and sports facilities.

Modern sculptures outside the La Défense office buildings in Paris.

Paris is home to many splendid monuments. The first were by the kings of France: Louis XIV had *Les Invalides*, for example, built as a home for soldiers invalided out of the army. In 1887-89 the Eiffel Tower was built to celebrate the hundredth anniversary of the French Revolution. The Presidents of France have continued the tradition begun by the kings they replaced. In 1969 Georges Pompidou launched the centre for contemporary art which is today called the Pompidou Centre. The building has all the water pipes and the ducts that carry cables on the outside.

The current president, President Mitterand, has devoted billions of francs to ambitious architectural projects. The *Pyramide du Louvre*, made of glass in the shape of an Egyptian pyamid, is the new entrance to the Louvre Museum. A new Opera House has been developed at the *Place de la Bastille*. In 1989 the *Arche de la Défense* was completed. This office complex made of white marble is an extension of the triumphal way which extends from the Louvre and the *Champs Elysées* through the *Arc de Triomphe* to the office complex at La Défense. To these monuments President Mitterand intends to add a new National Library designed by some of the world's leading architects. He says he wants to help France's cultural life: his critics accuse him of self glorification.

The most startling home to French service industries is La Défense in Paris. There, an extraordinary group of high-rise office blocks are used as the headquarters of major companies, banks and insurance companies.

40

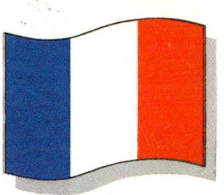

Daily life

A French family enjoys a drink outside before having Sunday lunch.

OWNERSHIP OF CONSUMER GOODS IN FRANCE, 1990	
Car	77%
Television	95%
Colour television	88%
Refrigerator	98%
Washing machine	87%
Dishwasher	30%
Telephone	94%
Microwave oven	18%

THE FAMILY

The family plays an important role in French life. Most French people (63.6 per cent in 1990) live in traditional families with two parents. This is becoming less common: fewer people are getting married, and more marriages are breaking up than ever before. This means that the number of one-parent families and people who live alone has increased. In the mid-1980s 15 per cent of children under 19 years of age lived in one-parent families.

HOUSING

French people earn and spend a lot of money, much of it on their homes. These are usually quite small, often with only three rooms. One of the reasons for this is that in cities French people tend to live in apartments. Individual houses with gardens are found mainly at the edges of towns.

FOOD

As well as housing, people spend a lot of money on food: about 20 per cent of what they earn. This is less than in the past. There have been changes recently in the types of food people buy. As they become more health conscious the French are eating less foods like sugar, butter, potatoes and meat. Instead they buy things like margarine and fish.

Each part of the country has its own regional specialities. In the north are rich pastures where cattle are raised, and butter and milk products are widely used. Among the apple-growing regions of Normandy ciders and delicious apple tarts are popular. In the hot south goats were for a long time the main source of meat and cheese, while olive oil is still an important basic cooking material.

There is still a strong interest in *haute cuisine* (carefully cooked food prepared by chefs who have spent years learning how to cook). Some of the leading chefs become famous personalities. The French probably still eat a greater variety of good food than people in any other European country.

A fruit and vegetable market in the town of Lalinde. Markets are common in France, and are a popular place to buy fresh food.

EDUCATION

Until they are 16 all French children have to attend school. There they learn traditional subjects such as maths and geography, as well as subjects like sewing and metalwork.

Up until the age of 16 children learn to read, write and speak well, to present logical arguments, and are taught some general knowledge. At 16 they can leave school or go on to a *lycée* for 2 years, to study for the *baccalauréat*. Anyone who passes this can go to university. Today more than half of school leavers take the *baccalauréat*. As well as *lycées*, young people can go on to technical schools to qualify as electricians, plumbers or mechanics.

At the end of the school day teachers and pupils go home. Few schools have orchestras, drama groups or school newspapers.

The famous Ecole Normale Supérieure, which trains academics who may one day be professors of literature and science. In the early 1990s there were more than a million students in France. Ninety per cent went to universities and the rest to technical colleges and grandes écoles.

HIGHER EDUCATION

Higher education is divided between the universities and the *grandes écoles*. Anyone who passes the *baccalauréat* can go to university, but when they get there they often find that the university does not have good facilities. Classes are often large, and many students drop out after one year. Others hang on until they get their first university qualification, after two years, then leave.

There are also 150 *grandes écoles*; only 5 per cent of students manage to get into these schools. To get in you have to spend an extra two years in a *lycée* to prepare for the special entrance exams. These are fiercely competitive. Conditions in the *grandes écoles* are much better than in the universities. Students work in small groups, have close contact with their teachers, and will find it easy to get a job when they leave.

The future

France is a wealthy country and will continue to be rich in the years to come. As for other rich countries, the last twenty years have been very difficult, and there have been changes in the type of employment people can get and how hard they are expected to work. However, France has developed very modern transport and telecommunications networks, and has

Although France is a wealthy country, it shares the problem of unemployment with other developed nations. People still buy fish, but increased mechanization means that the children of the fishermen below are unlikely to be able to work in the fishing industry.

redeveloped its major cities: both of these things will help industry and employment. France has also invested in electronics and other high-technology industries, and in the education and skills of its people. Should world economic conditions improve, France will be in a strong position to take advantage of them.

Nevertheless problems remain. Unemployment, poverty and crime are major challenges for France. There is going to be a very large increase in traffic congestion, which will lead to more air pollution.

France is also likely to see an increase in tourist development, and the cities will expand. At the same time rural populations will fall, as will the number of farmers and the amount of farmland. As more and more industrial robots are used, there will be less need for human workers and unemployment could rise.

The cathedral looms above the ancient city of Rouen. In the future France's cities seem likely to continue to grow, and its rural population likely to shrink.

France's future will depend on whether attempts are made to control these trends. If they continue, environmental problems and unemployment will increase, and the quality of life for many people will decline. If they are controlled people could work less, and have more free time and an improved quality of living.

In the wider world France seems likely to continue as a powerful member of the European Union, while keeping its unique culture, language and identity intact.

'Garges, like many big French city suburbs, is a 1960s concrete jungle with nothing to offer its young, multi-ethnic population. Nearly half of its 40,000 inhabitants are under 25, and of these nearly 30 per cent are unemployed.'
Guardian, *18 March 1994.*
Rioting broke out in Garges, a suburb of Paris, in March 1994.

Glossary

Bourgeoisie People such as lawyers, accountants, shopkeepers and business owners, who are usually more wealthy than manual workers.

Chef A head cook who works in a hotel or restaurant. Chefs have often undergone years of training.

Colony A territory controlled by another country.

Divine Right The idea, common in the Middle Ages, that kings and queens had been given their jobs by god.

Ducts A channel or tube along which cables or water are carried.

Empire A country's territories overseas, which it governs in order to make a profit from them.

Equality The idea that all people should have equal rights, and that no one should be treated differently for any reason (for example the colour of their skin or their religion).

Fraternity The French word *fraternite* is often translated as brotherhood. It refers to the idea that people should behave to each other as though they were related, with kindness and generosity.

Industrialization The change from most people in a country working in agriculture to industry being the main form of employment.

Ottoman Empire Based in what is now Turkey, the Ottoman Empire at one time controlled large areas of Europe, the Middle East and Africa. It allied itself with Germany during the First World War (1914-1918), and when the war ended the empire was defeated and broken up.

Philosopher A person who tries to provide others with ways of understanding the world.

Plateau A raised, flat area of land.

Population density The number of people living in an area of land. For example, a population density of 50/km² would mean that there was an average of 50 people living in each square kilometre.

Racism Treating someone badly because they are not white-skinned.

Rural In the countryside, outside towns.

Schists Plates of rock in which several different layers are visible.

Social security Financial help from the government for people who are ill, old or have lost their jobs.

Urban In built-up areas where a lot of people live.

Welfare State The part of the government that provides social security, public education and health services.

Further Information

BOOKS

Information books
Countries of the World – France   Alan Blackwood and Brigitte Chooson (Wayland 1988)
Country Fact File – France   Bussolin (Simon and Schuster 1994)
On the Map – France   Ian James (Watts 1988)
Our Country – France   Julia Powell (Wayland 1990)
World in View – France   (Macmillan Children's Books 1989)
Usborne First Book of France   L Somerville (Usborne 1993)

FILMS

Two of the most famous recent French films are *Jean de Florette* and *Manon de Sources*, which together tell the story of a family's attempt to start a farm in Provence. They're quite long, but contain wonderful shots of the hill country of the south of France. The films are based on two novels by Marcel Pagnol.

Another great French film is *Cyrano de Bergerac*, based on the play by Edmond Rostand. It tells the rip-roaring tale of Cyrano, a famous French writer and soldier. Each of these films should be available on video.

PICTURE ACKNOWLEDGEMENTS
Grateful thanks to the following for allowing their photographs to be reproduced in this book: Bryan and Cherry Alexander 44 (bottom); Cephas 22, 23 (both), 26, 29, 41; Robert Estall 30, 42; Explorer, Paris title page, 4, 6, 8, 11, 16, 32, 33, 34, 35, 39, 40 (bottom); Eye Ubiquitous 21, 40 (top); Hughes-Gilby contents page; Impact 17, 20 (both); Rex Features/ Sipa Press 14, 18, 19, 24, 25; Tony Stone Images 10 (top), 13, 36; Wayland 9 (both), 43, 44, 45.

Index

aerospace   32
agriculture   8, 13, 26, 27, 28, 29
Algeria   9, 19
Alps, French   11, 32
Ardennes   10
Atlantic Ocean   10, 11, 12

Belgium   10
Bordeaux   11, 13, 19, 38
Brittany   10, 12, 17, 28

cities   12, 19, 21, 22, 31
   see Paris
civil service   14
climate   12
Colonial Empire   6, 7, 8
communes   15, 16
constitution   14
cooperatives   26

democratic   16
départements   16
Dordogne   11

education   15, 33, 42, 43
Eiffel Tower   4, 39
employment   21, 27
energy resources   31
Europe   4, 7, 10, 12, 17, 26, 29
European trade   6
European Union   45

farmers   26, 29, 45
farming   8, 26, 27
First World War   4, 32
food   26, 42

Germany   8, 10, 26, 32
government   9, 14, 16
   local   15, 16
   ministries   14
   national   14, 15
   regional   15

immigrants   18, 20, 23, 24
industry   7-9, 21, 22, 24, 29, 31-33, 45
Italy   6, 10, 11, 19, 35

Jura   11

Lake Geneva   12
Laos   19
laws   25
Le Havre   13
Luxembourg   10

Marseille   34
Massif Central   11, 13, 28
Mediterranean   10, 12, 13, 28, 32
mining   13
Minister   25
Mitterand, President   25, 40
monarchy   14, 38
monuments   39, 40
Morocco   19
mountains   10, 12

Nantes   11, 13
National Centre for Space Research   32
Normandy   12, 17, 28, 42
North Sea   10
nuclear power   31

Paris   6, 11, 19, 20, 22, 32, 34, 37, 39
Paris Basin   10, 27
pollution   13, 35
   air   13, 45
   water   13
Pompidou Centre   39
poor   23
population   5, 7, 13, 17-19, 31, 36, 39, 45
Pyrenees   10, 11

racism   20
regions   16
revolution   14, 15, 27, 28, 37, 38
riots   24
rivers   11
   Loire   11
   Rhine   10
   Rhône   12, 13
   Saône   13
   Seine   11
rural areas   13, 29, 31

Second World War   8, 22, 32
services   22
   transport   31
Spain   10, 11, 17, 19
suburbs   24, 39
Switzerland   10-12

Toulouse   13, 19, 32, 33
tourism and leisure   31, 32, 45
trade   6
traffic   35
transport   34
   métro   35
   railway system   34
   water   35
Tunisia   19

unemployment   20, 22-24
United Nations Security Council   4
Urban Renewal Programme   25
USA   26

Vietnam   9, 19

wealth   23
weather   12
Welfare State   9, 46